M000224145

Billy, the Boy Who Had to Wear Glasses

By Pauline Cartwright

Illustrated by Mario Capaldi

DOMINIE PRESS

Pearson Learning Group

Publisher: Raymond Yuen
Project Editor: John S. F. Graham
Editor: Bob Rowland
Designer: Greg DiGenti
Illustrator: Mario Capaldi

Text Copyright © 2003 Pauline Cartwright
Illustrations Copyright © 2003 Dominie Press, Inc.
All rights reserved. No part of this publication may
be reproduced or transmitted in any form or by any
means without permission in writing from the publisher.
Reproduction of any part of this book, through photocopy,
recording, or any electronic or mechanical retrieval system,
without the written permission of the publisher, is an
infringement of the copyright law.

Published by:

℮ Dominie Press, Inc.

1949 Kellogg Avenue
Carlsbad, California 92008 USA

www.dominie.com

1-800-232-4570

Paperback ISBN 0-7685-1624-2
Printed in Singapore
   4 5 6   10 09 08 07

Table of Contents

Chapter One
You Need Glasses

Billy's mother took him to the eye doctor. She took him there because she was worried about his eyes. She thought that Billy might not see things very well.

"Billy," said the eye doctor, "you need glasses. Then you'll see things better."

"You're just like your dad," his mother said. "He's been wearing glasses for years."

Billy didn't say anything as they walked home. He was imagining himself wearing glasses. It made him feel so awful that his eyes filled with tears. He couldn't see where he was going, and he almost banged his head on a lamppost.

"Oh, dear," said his mother. "It's a good thing we went to the eye doctor. You really *do* need glasses."

Billy had to wait a week for his new glasses. He moped around the house until his mother shooed him outside to go for a walk.

Chapter Two

I'd Punch Them in the Nose!

Billy met Hunter, the rabbit, running around a wheat field.

"Hey, stop!" Billy called. "I want to ask you something."

Hunter stopped running around the field, but his feet didn't stop going up and down.

"Hunter, if you had to wear glasses and everyone teased you and laughed at you, what would you do?" asked Billy.

Hunter started hopping around, boxing his paws in the air.

"I'd tell them off!" said Hunter. "That's what I'd do! I'd punch them in the nose!

Wham! Bang! Wham! Then I'd run away fast, just like I'm going to do now."

And off he went back to running around the wheat field.

That night, Billy hopped around in his room, punching his fists in the air. He pretended to feel fierce, but he was only pretending. He didn't want to hit his friends. He didn't even want to hit people he didn't like.

Chapter Three

I'm Just Not Very Brave

The next day, Billy saw Tessie, the cow, dreaming in the corner of a field.

"Hey," he called. "I want to ask you something."

Tessie looked up when Billy got close.

"Tessie, if you had to wear glasses and

everyone teased you and laughed at you, what would you do?" asked Billy.

Tessie looked at Billy with her big brown eyes. She smiled a gentle smile. "I'd probably cry," she said. "When people hurt my feelings, I cry."

Billy saw that her eyes were filling up with tears.

"I don't want to upset you, Tessie," he said. "I'm sorry I asked."

"That's all right," said Tessie, blinking the tears away. "I'm just not very brave."

Billy knew he wasn't as brave as some of his friends, but he thought he was braver than Tessie.

Chapter Four
I Would Hide

Later that day, Billy's mother sent him on an errand to the store. Ahead of him on the path, he saw Edward, the sheep, wandering along.

"Wait for me! I want to ask you something," Billy shouted. He ran and

caught up with Edward. "Edward, if you had to wear glasses and everyone teased you and laughed at you, what would you do?"

Edward lifted his head to look at Billy. He said gloomily, "I would hide. I'd go up into the hills, where no one could annoy me. Then I'd get on with what I wanted to do."

"It wouldn't be much fun having no one to talk to," said Billy.

Edward sniffed a small sniff. "I've never really had much fun, anyway," he said.

Billy decided he'd get very gloomy himself if he talked very long with Edward. He went on his way.

Chapter Five
I'd Be Really Rude

Out of the trees stepped Maddie, the cat. Billy stopped to talk. "If you had to wear glasses and everyone teased you and laughed at you, what would you do?" Billy asked Maddie.

Maddie sprang up close to him and

hissed. "If anyone laughed at me, for any
reason at all, I'd be really rude. I'd hiss
and spit and call them all kinds of
terrible names. I can teach you many
rude names. Would you like me to teach
them to you?"

"No, thank you," said Billy. "No one
would like me if I called them rude

names. They won't like you, either," he told Maddie.

"So what if they don't like me," hissed Maddie. "I don't care."

"Everyone needs friends," said Billy.

He left Maddie to practice angry spits by herself and went on home.

Chapter Six
A Whole Lot Better

In a few days, a package came in the mail.

"Look!" said Billy's mother. "I think it's your new glasses."

"I don't want to wear glasses," said Billy.

"Don't be so stubborn," said his

mother. "Try them on. See if they make everything clearer."

Billy took his glasses outside before he put them on. He didn't want anyone to see him with them on, not even his mother.

He put on the glasses and was very surprised. The flowers looked brighter. The clouds looked fluffier. The hills looked grassier, and the water looked splashier.

"Come in and show your dad," called

his mother.

Billy went back inside, like gloomy Edward, the sheep, and sighed.

Billy's father looked up from his stamp collection. "New glasses!" he said. "They look pretty good. I'll bet you can see everything a whole lot better, now."

"Yes." Billy had to agree. "I can. But I'm scared that people will laugh at me, and I don't know what to do. Dad, what do you do when people laugh at your glasses?"

"I've never noticed anyone laughing at me," said his father. "Have you seen anyone laughing at me?"

Billy thought for a moment. "No," he said. "I haven't."

"There you go," said his father, and he went back to his stamps. Billy stared around the room. The walls looked shinier.

The stamps looked more interesting.

"If they did laugh," said his father suddenly, "I'd just ignore them, anyway. I'm glad I can see better with my glasses on. If I couldn't see my stamps, I wouldn't be able to enjoy them as much."

Billy thought his father looked wiser than ever. He went back outside and kept looking at the world through his new glasses. The leaves looked greener. The rocks looked rockier.

Later, dinner looked yummier. His friends looked friendlier, maybe because one of them said, "Your glasses look great!"

Another one said, "I'm glad you can see everything better now."

Nobody laughed at all. And Billy now knew that if anyone did, it really wouldn't matter at all.